D Double fun: You + I

E Experiences Genuine

F Freshness + Free Time

K "Karrots" + Herbal Tea

L Love + Air

M Muesli + Ocean

ke + del

Q Quiet spring water + Goofing around

R Rest + Slide

S Soup + Singing

W

us

X Xylophone + Joy XXL

Y Yin + Yang

Z ZZZs to catch

Zip + Pep after getting better

Visit our website at www.skyponypress.com.

10 9 8 7 6 5 4 3 2 1

Manufactured in China, June 2022
This product conforms to CPSIA 2008

Library of Congress Cataloging-in-Publication Data is available on file.

Cover design by Elke Kohlmann
Cover illustrations by Dagmar Geisler
US Edition edited by Nicole Frail

Print ISBN: 978-1-5107-7095-9
Ebook ISBN: 978-1-5107-7096-6

When I Get Sick

About Becoming Ill and Feeling Better

Written and Illustrated by Dagmar Geisler
Translated by Andy Berasaluce

Sky Pony Press
New York

Have you ever been sick? Or are you sick right now?

Everybody gets sick sometimes.

There are sicknesses almost everyone knows about. Most people have had a cough or a cold. But there are also a lot of other illnesses. Many are contagious. They are caused by viruses or by bacteria. Both are teeny tiny and invisible to the naked eye.

I have a cough and a cold.

I have an earache.

I just beat cancer.

I have chicken pox.

I have a tummy ache.

A VIRUS

A virus is even smaller than a bacterium. Viruses can only transfer from one living being to another. The viruses sit, let's say, in the spit of someone sick with the flu. When someone sneezes or coughs, the tiny droplets can fly out pretty far. That's why you should sneeze and cough into a tissue. Or, when you don't have a tissue, into the inside of your elbow.

A BACTERIUM

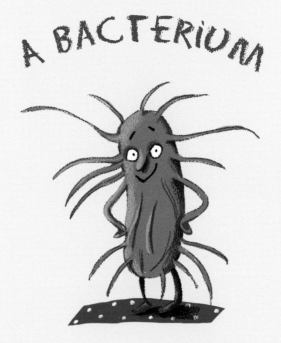

Bacteria are bigger. Bacteria don't necessarily need a living being to spread. They can be found, for instance, in spoiled food or dirty water. They might cause tummy aches or diarrhea.

Some examples of contagious illnesses are:

cold with a cough and sniffles   Measles   Chicken pox

Rubella   The flu   Scarlet Fever   Fifth disease

Many illnesses aren't contagious. They develop because something in the body doesn't work like it should. This can happen for several different reasons. But these have nothing to do with viruses and bacteria. That's why you don't have be scared of catching them.

Some examples of illnesses that aren't contagious:

Diabetes   Eczema   Asthma

Cancer   Mental Illnesses
(for example, depression)   Allergies

Spit droplets (with one enormously enlarged)

Matt has a cough and the sniffles. The virus is in his spit and breath. Izzy doesn't notice that, along with fresh air, she's breathing in a little of Matt's spit.

It really isn't that easy. Our bodies have an immune system. There are guards within us on the lookout for something coming from outside that could harm us. And they are quite good at their jobs. Viruses and bacteria are always within us and all around us. The guards in our bodies recognize the ones that are good for us. By the way, that's most of them. And they recognize the ones that plan to make us sick.

When they detect that kind of intruder, they call for reinforcements and – whoosh! – the evildoer is rendered harmless.

WEE-OOH!

Guard cells sound the alarm.

Scavenger cells devour the intruder.

Immune cells fight the intruder.

That can happen for several reasons.

For example, it might be that an unusually high number of a type of pathogen is flying around. This sometimes happens during cold season. The guards might be busy with one enemy, so another slipped through their fingers.

And when you're not, for whatever reason, so healthy, perhaps the guards then are also a little tired.

To reduce the risk of infection, there are some things we can do on our own: Washing your hands often is good. Since we touch so much with our hands, it's very possible that, in doing so, we can catch something that makes us sick.

Bring on the soap and water!

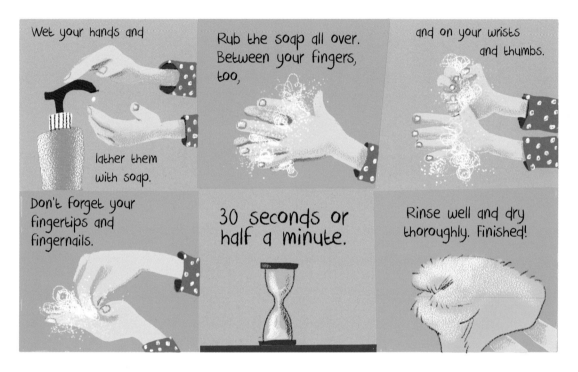

Wet your hands and lather them with soap.

Rub the soap all over. Between your fingers, too,

and on your wrists and thumbs.

Don't forget your fingertips and fingernails.

30 seconds or half a minute.

Rinse well and dry thoroughly. Finished!

When coughing or sneezing, don't get too close to others. Use a tissue, or, if necessary, the inside of your elbow.

At times when an especially high number of viruses are around, it's good to wear a surgical mask.

Izzy didn't get sick. But the viruses that she breathed in jumped over to Tarik. That can happen even when Izzy stays healthy.

Now Tarik has a sore throat, cough, headache, and runny nose. He has a cold, for sure. His body's defenses are working now at full blast. They are capably heating up the virus. Tarik gets a mild fever.

Viruses don't like heat, which is why the fever helps fight them off. This fight is very demanding on the body. To heal quickly, Tarik needs peace and quiet from everyone. Tarik snuggles into bed, and when his headache isn't so bad anymore, Dad will read him a story.

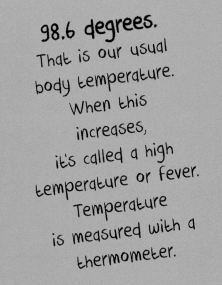

98.6 degrees.
That is our usual body temperature. When this increases, it's called a high temperature or fever. Temperature is measured with a thermometer.

Sleep is good. Then the immune system can work in peace.

A warm compress helps with a sore throat.

Tissues and ointment for the red sniffly nose.

Tarik has no appetite for food right now. That's totally fine. The body needs a lot of strength for digestion.

But it's very important to drink a lot. That way fighting the germs goes very smoothly. Herbal tea is good. Or just water.

Tarik is lucky. With lots of rest and a few home remedies, he quickly recovers. Home remedies are things everyone can have at home that can help with illness or minor injuries.

Onions help with earaches or are good for coughs.

Hot water bottles and chamomile tea help with stomachaches.

Ice packs help for bumps and bruises.

Sage tea and warm compresses help with a sore throat.

Herbal ointment for chest congestion.

BAND-AIDS

A warm bag of cherry stones works for backaches.

And if none of that helps?

If the fever or pain is too severe or lasts too long, then people see a doctor. Like Greta, who is going with her father to a doctor. At the doctor's, first there's an examination. The doctor takes a close look at Greta and asks where it hurts and how she feels. The signs that she discovers tell her what illness Greta has. Doctors call such signs symptoms.

Some of the signs, the doctor can see.

Some she can hear.

For some examinations, she looks inside the body. There are devices for this, for example, an ultrasound, as shown in the picture below, or an X-ray machine.

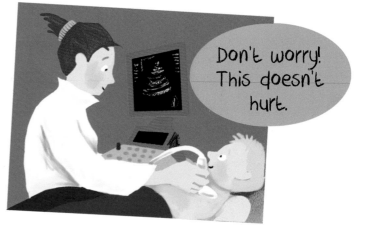

Don't worry! This doesn't hurt.

Other signs she recognizes in her patients' blood or urine. The blood is taken from the arm with a syringe. One small prick and it's over.

For the urine tests, you pee into a cup. For Greta, it's not necessary this time. The doctor immediately recognized that she had chicken pox. She writes a prescription for the medicines Dad is supposed to get from the pharmacy. She explains to Greta what type of illness it is. She tells her how long to stay at home in bed and what she can do to make the bumps on her skin no longer itch.

The doctor is very knowledgeable about most diseases. She's a general practitioner. But because there are so many different diseases and injuries, we also need doctors who are especially familiar with other parts of the body. There are ear, nose, and throat doctors, dermatologists and dentists, doctors who know everything about our bones, and many other specialists.

The general practitioner can tell whether she needs to refer her patient to a specialist, and she also knows which specialist is the right one.

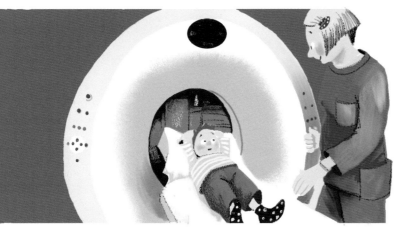

Max is sent to the hospital. At the hospital, there are also a lot of specialists and special devices, like a computerized X-ray machine, which can photograph everything inside Max's belly.

Max's general practitioner already suspected Max had appendicitis, and it's true. Here in the hospital, he can have the operation shortly after the examination.

Max didn't notice the operation at all. Beforehand, he received an anesthetic. This means that he simply slept during the operation and didn't feel any pain. When Max woke up, it was all over, and there was a bandage over the wound on his stomach. It still pinches, but the bad stomachache is over. How lucky!

Max is supposed to stay in the hospital for a few more days. He stays in a hospital room where two other children already are. "Did you have appendicitis too?" asks Max.

Mila has been in the hospital for a few weeks. She had cancer, so first she had an operation and then came chemotherapy. This finally beat the cancer cells. The hair that had fallen out as a result is growing back, and soon Mila will be able to go home again.

Greg didn't need an operation. He has a disease called diabetes. The doctors at the hospital want to look into what he needs to live successfully with his illness.

Greg, Mila, and Max all have different illnesses. But they have something in common: diabetes, cancer, and appendicitis are not contagious.

What about our immune system then? Does it have anything to do with those types of diseases?

Our immune systems are always active.

Hello there!

We fight off everything that could harm the body.

We watch out so that something contagious from outside doesn't get in.

We deal with the cells that might become cancerous. We clear most of them away before they can make the person sick.

We keep learning and take a close look at every new pathogen. Then, the next time, we'll know how to defend ourselves. Some diseases, therefore, you can only catch once. After that, we have the matter under control.

By the way, this also happens with vaccination. For some diseases, vaccines exist. They contain a tiny amount of the disease's pathogens. Just enough for us, the immune cells, to get familiar with it. We make sure that you can no longer get sick from this type of pathogen. Then you can say: I'm immune to this disease.

But we can't do all of this alone. Luckily, there are doctors and hospitals and medicines and a lot of other health helpers.

WE WORK TOGETHER!

Exactly!

Some drugs and treatments work so strongly that things also happen in the body that aren't actually necessary to fight the disease. This is very exhausting for the body. It could cause you to feel sick or, like Mila, cause hair to fall out. There are also diseases that never go away completely. Greg's diabetes is one of them. Greg has what's called a chronic illness. When you can't get rid of a disease, it's necessary to find a way to live with it.

People who have diseases like that learn to take good care of themselves. They know what they can and can't eat. They know when they have to be careful when playing and when it's better to relax. Anyone who wants to help can support them. There's no reason to laugh at someone or not to let them play with you.

I have diabetes. I'm missing a substance called insulin. I have to pay attention to what I eat. I've learned how to give myself an insulin shot. I also measure how much sugar I have in my blood. I have everything I need to do so in my bag.

I had cancer. That's why I was in the hospital for a long time. Now my hair's growing back. Sometimes I'm still tired. Later on, I want to become a clown because clowns came to visit the clinic. That was great!

My friend has cancer, too. He's pretty weak at the moment. Until we can play soccer together again, we trade soccer pictures.

I've been unable to walk since I was born. But I can dance. There's a wheelchair dance club in our city. I go there with my friend.

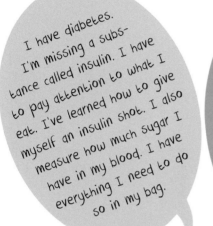

Some children are comfortable openly discussing about how they cope with illness. But you also may just ask. The more we know about ourselves and others, the better we get along. And then we'll have more fun, too. The fun doesn't stop just because someone has an illness.

I have eczema. The spots on my skin itch, but they aren't contagious. When it's especially bad, it makes me nervous. And then some-times everything becomes too much for me.

I have a heart defect. That's why some things are too strenuous for me. I then have to take a break. But when I build my ships, I have a lot of endurance.

I have an allergy to hazelnuts. I even had to go to the hospital because of just one. That was hard because I missed a basketball game. I'm pretty good at basketball.

I have asthma. That's why sometimes I have a hard time breathing. This spray helps with that. I always have it with me.

Mom was in the hospital. Now she's at home but must sleep a lot. We have to keep very quiet.

Sick people need our understanding, our help, and our consideration. And rightfully so.

I've learned to make Mom's favorite salad. With carrots, honey, and nuts. It's not very hard.

Since my brother got sick, Mom and Dad are often sad and afraid for him. Me too. But sometimes I'd like for them to play with me again. Is it even alright to think like that?

Sometimes I'm really angry because Lisa gets so many things now, even though it's not her birthday.

I'd very much like to invite my friends over again and goof around, like before.

Sometimes I'm in a horribly bad mood. I can hardly stand that everyone's so nice to me. I'd love to stick my tongue out at them.

The other day I was at the swimming pool with my friends, and we giggled the whole time. It was so fun.

But am I allowed to have fun when Mom''s so sick?

Above all, when someone we love is sick, we want to do everything we can to make them feel better.

My brother's sickness scares me. But Mom and Dad are so sad already, I'd never dare tell them.

We want to be nice and friendly and are sometimes very surprised when we also have different feelings. It's totally normal. Feelings are always a part of life, even those feelings we don't like so much.

It's not about never being in a bad mood again. It's about not taking it out on someone else.

It helps to talk about your feelings. You can even say: "I'm in a wretched mood today and don't even know why." Then you can better understand each other.

And it helps to do something to get rid of the bad feeling, like a fun afternoon. That makes us stronger, and those who are strong can cope much better in difficult times. This goes for both healthy and sick people.

The time when someone's sick can be very stressful. That's why it is sometimes good to let yourself receive help.
Your family may need help with practical things like shopping or homework. And sometimes you also need someone you can talk to about everything.

Yes, that's right. Sometimes someone loses the fight against the disease and dies. That's very sad. Especially for those who loved this person. And also for the doctors and nurses who tried everything to keep them alive.

Our mother died. At first, it hurt so much we could hardly stand it. We cried a lot, Dad, Lisa, and I. It still hurts, but now every day we write down all the things we did and fold the notes into paper boats. She used to like these so much. Sometimes we can actually laugh. And then Mom's still a little bit with us somehow.

LUCA

Dear Mama, Today we went to the pool.

MOM

We miss you.

LISA

I kan rite now mama

DAD

Today the sun was shining

Illness and dying are part of life. Sadly, that's how it is. But we have to remember that doctors and nurses are learning just as much as our immune cells.

Lots of diseases that people used to die from are no longer a problem for our heroes of defense. And if a new illness comes along, they immediately start learning again. They learn faster each time, because they are already so experienced.

This is the case, for example, when there's a new virus in the world that no one knows about and with which many people become infected very quickly. This is called an epidemic or, if the contagion spreads around the world, a pandemic. Right away, medical professionals begin researching this new virus, and our immune cells are already busy getting familiar with it and fighting it. And we can do something, too.

Our immune systems are always there for us. They do their best. For them to work well, we need to give them what keeps them alert and makes them strong.

THESE MAKE US WEAK:

too many fries, burgers, chips, etc.

too many sweets

too much hanging around

too much stress

And what else helps with staying healthy?

Having fun and playing.
Goofing around with friends
and laughing and being happy.

And what
does you good?

Advice and Help

APA.org
American Psychological Association
750 First Street, NE
Washington, District of Columbia 20002
Phone: (202) 336-5500
Toll-Free: (800) 374-2721

ChildCare.gov
Office of Child Care
US Department of Health and Human Services
Administration for Children and Families
Mary E. Switzer Building
330 C ST SW, 4th floor
Washington, DC 20201
Phone Number: (202) 690-6782
Email: ChildCare.gov@acf.hhs.gov

ChildTraumaAcademy.org
ChildTrauma Academy
5161 San Felipe
Suite 320
Houston, Texas 77056-3646
Phone: (281) 932-1375
Email: ChildTrauma@ChildTraumaAcademy.org

ChildrensCancer.org
Children's Cancer Research Fund
7301 Ohms Lane, Suite 355
Minneapolis, MN 55439
Phone: 952-893-9355
Email: contact@childrenscancer.org

ChildrensHeartLink.org
Children's HeartLink
5075 Arcadia Avenue
Minneapolis, MN 55436
Phone: 952-928-4860
Email: hello@childrensheartlink.org

HealthyChildren.org
American Academy of Pediatrics
345 Park Boulevard
Itasca, IL 60143
Phone Number: (630) 626-6000
Email: info@healthychildren.org

Healthy Teen Network
1501 St. Paul Street
Suite 114
Baltimore, Maryland 21202
Phone: (410) 685-0410
Email: Info@HealthyTeenNetwork.org

HHS.gov
The U.S. Department of Health & Human Services
Hubert H. Humphrey Building
200 Independence Avenue, S.W.
Washington, D.C. 20201
Toll Free Call Center: 1-877-696-6775

KidsWishNetwork.org
Kids Wish Network
301 Bear Ridge Circle
Palm Harbor, Florida 34683
Phone: 1-866-990-0108
Email: info@kidswishnetwork.org

Afterword

At the very beginning of this book, I wrote: "Illness is a part of life." And it is. None of us would like to get sick or be sick, and yet it happens again and again. Children, especially, get infections, a sign that their immune system is in its learning phase. The immune system becomes familiar with all types of pathogens, and thus acquires the ability to defend itself against them.

I learned a lot about the miracle of the body's defenses while researching this book. It's true that anything truly good for us makes our defenses stronger. This applies to nutrition as well as exercise and, in a special way, to positive experiences.

I once read a study on an experiment with actors. When the actors played a scene with happy feelings, one could detect more activity from the immune cells than when they performed something sad. How much more effective must that be when it comes to feelings in real life?

My favorite topic of "**feelings and how they affect us**" also comes into play here. When we treat each other well, it also helps our health. I like that.

Dagmar Geisler

Dagmar Geisler has already supported several generations of parents in accompanying their children through emotionally difficult situations. With her picture book series, Safe Child, Happy Parent, the author and illustrator sensitively deals with the most important topics related to growing up: from body awareness to exploring one's own emotional world to social interaction. Her work always includes a helping of humor. Even when things get serious—then even more so. Her books have been translated into 20 languages.